快乐拼读

Happy Phonics

主编 朱舒陵

远方出版社

图书在版编目（CIP）数据

快乐拼读 Happy Phonics ／ 朱舒陵主编．-- 呼和浩特：远方出版社，2020.5

ISBN 978-7-5555-1459-6

Ⅰ．①快… Ⅱ．①朱… Ⅲ．①英语课－小学－教学参考资料 Ⅳ．① G624.313

中国版本图书馆 CIP 数据核字（2020）第 064388 号

快乐拼读 Happy Phonics
KUAILE PINDU

主　　编	朱舒陵
责任编辑	王　叶
责任校对	王　叶
装帧设计	王改英
出版发行	远方出版社
社　　址	呼和浩特市乌兰察布东路 666 号　邮编 010010
电　　话	（0471）2236473 总编室　2236460 发行部
经　　销	新华书店
印　　刷	内蒙古爱信达教育印务有限责任公司
开　　本	184mm×260mm　1/16
字　　数	100 千
印　　张	4.75
版　　次	2020 年 5 月第 1 版
印　　次	2020 年 5 月第 1 次印刷
标准书号	ISBN 978-7-5555-1459-6
定　　价	45.00 元

如发现印装质量问题，请与出版社联系调换

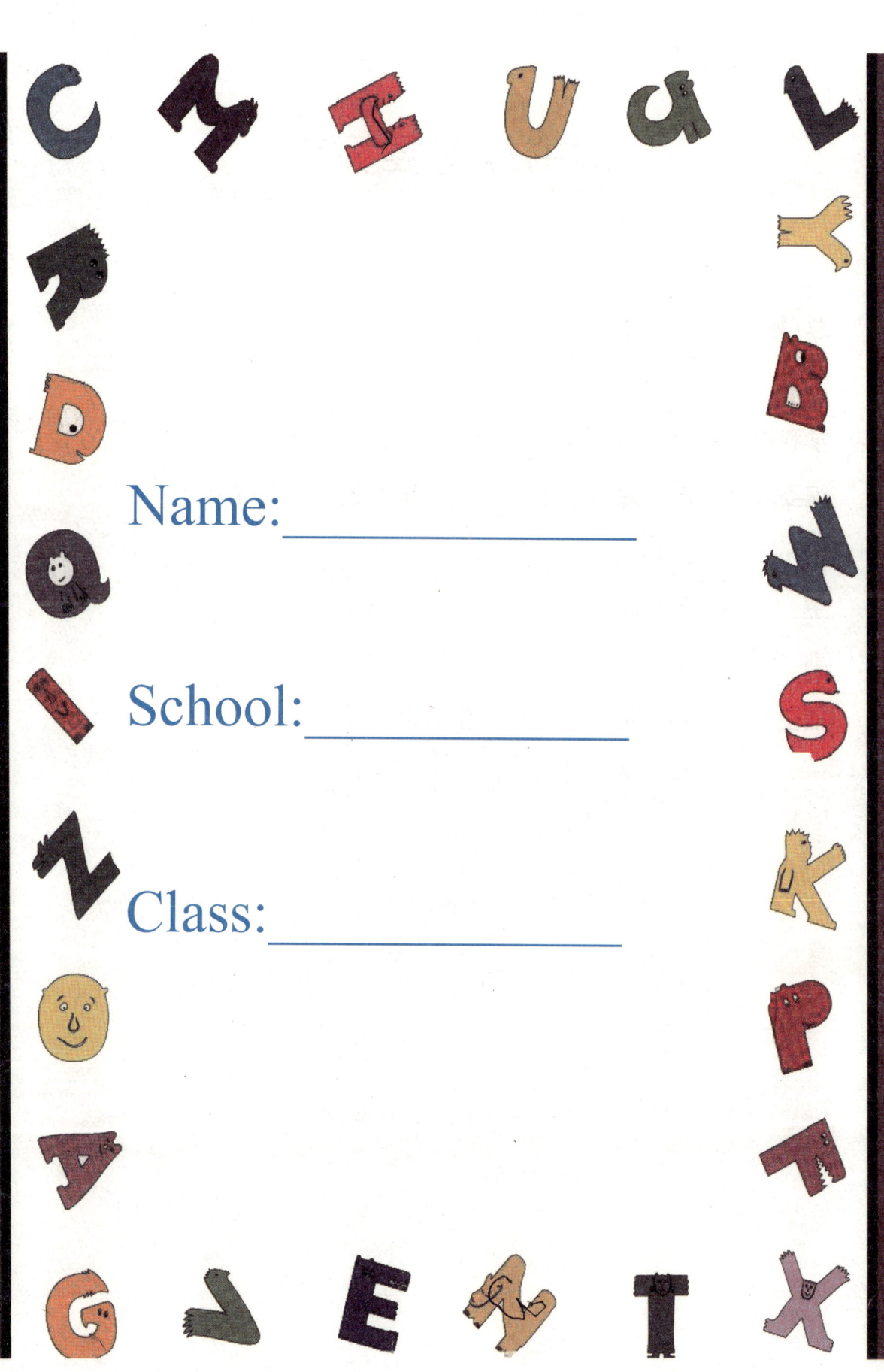

Name: _____

School: _____

Class: _____

本书编写委员会

总 顾 问：许光明
策　 　划：白兆丹
学科指导：章　全
编委成员：朱舒陵　万常倩　张　岚　董　涛　徐立新
　　　　　丁嘉欣
主　　编：朱舒陵
副 主 编：万常倩
插图编写：刘治文　王　琳　张若群　徐　敏　李　琪
　　　　　林　洁　孙长江

　　本书为铜陵市教育科学研究课题《基于教材重组，构建农村小学英语phonics教学"新课堂"的应用研究》（课题编号：tl2017029）专项研究成果。

前　言

　　在以英语为母语的国家，学生要用一年的学校教育时间来系统地学习26个字母的字母名（letter name）、字母音（letter sound）和拼读规则，然后在阅读中巩固强化这些规则。为此，编者在结合多年英语教学经验及与英国学校教师合作交流的基础上，通过精心设计、编撰、修改，编写了《快乐拼读 Happy Phonics》一书。本书的编排既遵循了英语学习的规律，又考虑到了中国学生的学习习惯。

　　全书分为4个单元，每个单元包括6~7个字母的教学以及复习，涉及26个字母的书写、字母名（letter name）、字母音（letter sound）、高频词（sight words）以及初级阅读。每一课内容包括4个部分：A. Let's learn（学习新的字母名和字母音）；B. Let's trace, write and say（学习书写）；C. Practice（各种形式的练习）；D. Let's listen and do（通过歌曲和动作拓展）。学习两课后，每一课加上Blending time（拼读练习）。复习课也包括4个部分：A. Match and write（复习书写）；B. Let's blend（复习拼读）；C. Let's read（学习高频词和阅读）；D. Let's play（通过各种游戏巩固所学知识）。

　　本书是针对零基础的学生设计的，充分考虑到了低年级学生的年龄特征，以激发和培养他们学习英语的兴趣为目的，为他们的终身学习和发展打下良好的基础。

编　者

LIST

Unit 1 S A T I P N

Ss → snake ·················· 1
Aa → apple ·················· 3
Tt → tennis ·················· 5
Ii → ink ·················· 7
Pp → panda ·················· 9
Nn → nose ·················· 11
Revision 1 ·················· 13

Unit 2 C K E H R M D

Cc/Kk → cat/kite ·················· 17
Ee → egg ·················· 19
Hh → hen ·················· 21
Rr → rabbit ·················· 23
Mm → mum ·················· 25
Dd → dad ·················· 27
Revision 2 ·················· 29

Unit 3 G O U L F B

Gg	→ gift	33
Oo	→ orange	35
Uu	→ umbrella	37
Ll	→ lollipop	39
Ff	→ fish	41
Bb	→ ball	43
Revision 3		45

Unit 4 J Z W V Y X Q

Jj	→ jelly	49
Zz	→ zoo	51
Ww	→ window	53
Vv	→ van	55
Yy	→ yogurt	57
Xx	→ X-ray	59
Qq	→ queen	61
Revision 4		63
Read for Fun		67

Unit1 S A T I P N

A. Let's learn.

S s
snake

s, s, S.
s, s, snake.

B. Let's trace, write and say.

C. Write S s, then listen and match.

D. Let's chant and do.

Hello, Snake. *s-s-s!*

Hello, Sun. *s-s-s!*

The snake is in the sun. *s-s-s!*

The snake is in the sun. *s-s-s!*

Action: Please move your body like a snake, and say *s, s, s*.

Unit1 SATIPN

A. Let's learn.

A a
apple

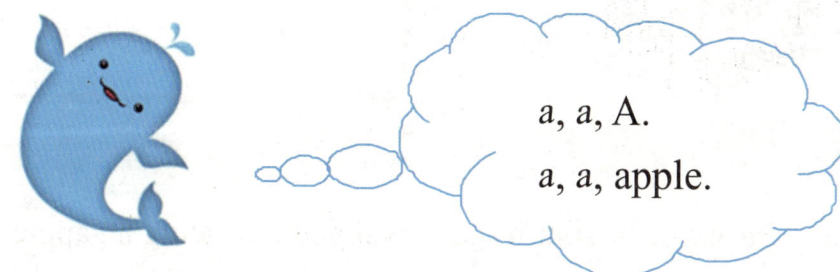

a, a, A.
a, a, apple.

B. Let's trace, write and say.

A a

C. Listen , match and write A a.

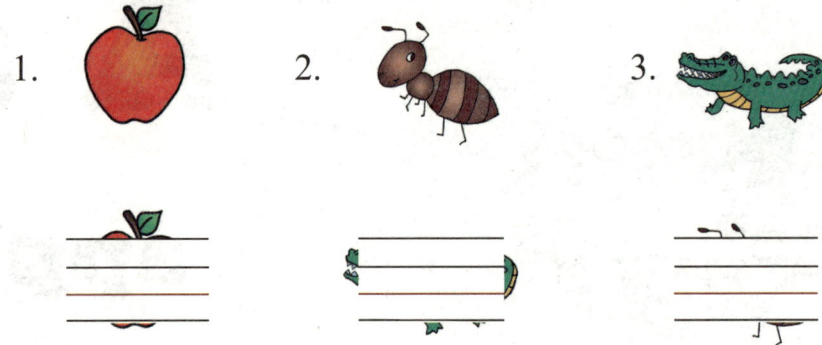

D. Let's chant and do.

Apple red, apple round.
Apple, apple, *a-a-a*.
I like apples. *a-a-a*.
I like apples. *a-a-a*.

Action: Please open your mouth, as if you are eating an apple, and say *a, a, a*.

Unit1 SA T IPN

A. Let's learn.

T t
tennis

t, t, T.
t, t, tennis.

B. Let's trace, write and say.

C. Listen and circle the words with the sound /t/.

1.   2.   3.

4.   5.

D. Let's listen and do.

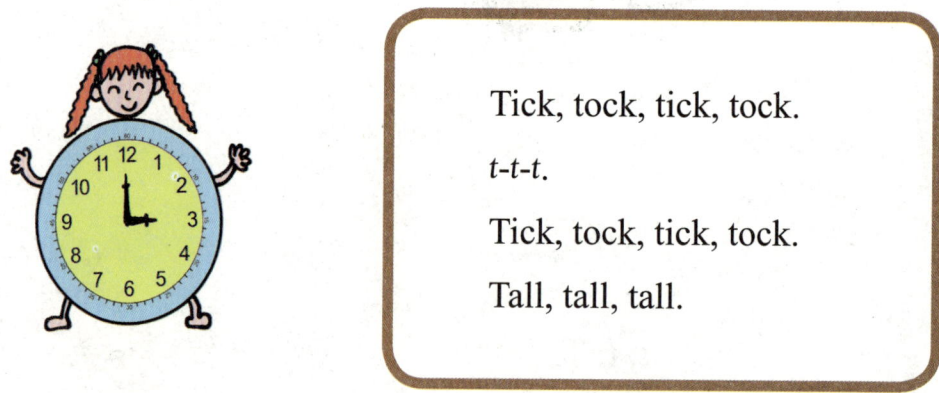

Tick, tock, tick, tock.

t-t-t.

Tick, tock, tick, tock.

Tall, tall, tall.

Action: Pretend to be a clock by moving your arms, like hour hand and minute hand, and say *t, t, t*.

Unit 1 SATIPN

Blending time.

A. Let's learn.

I i

ink

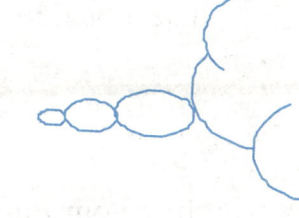

i, i, I.
i, i, ink.

B. Let's trace, write and say.

C. Write I i, then listen and match.

D. Let's listen and do.

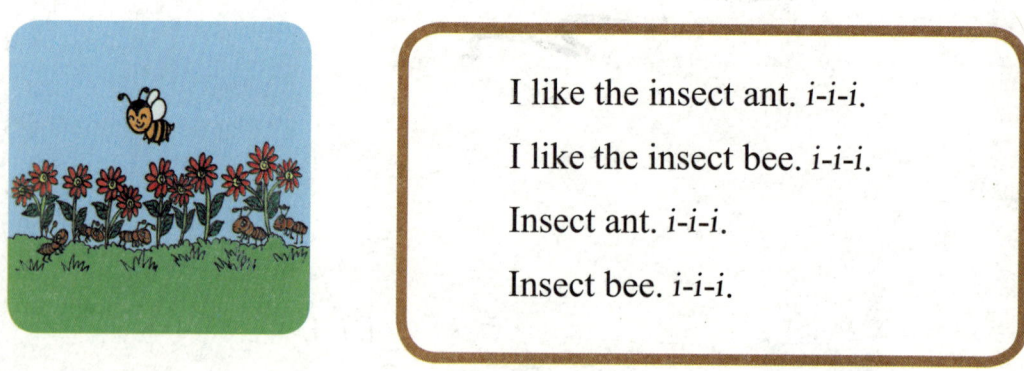

I like the insect ant. *i-i-i.*

I like the insect bee. *i-i-i.*

Insect ant. *i-i-i.*

Insect bee. *i-i-i.*

Action: Pretend to be an ant by wiggling your fingers, and say *i, i, i.*

Unit 1 SATI P N

Blending time.

A. Let's learn.

P p
panda

p, p, P.
p, p, panda.

B. Let's trace, write and say.

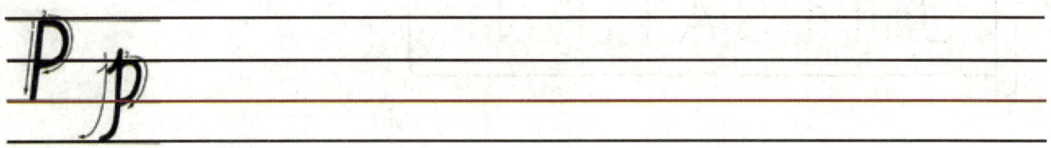

C. Which one begins with the sound /p/? Listen and circle.

1.

2.

3.

D. Let's chant and do.

What colour is the pig?
The pig is pink!
What colour is the cake?
The cake is pink!
The pink pig cake! *p-p-p*.

Action: Pretend to blow out the candles, and say *p, p, p*.

Unit 1 SATIPN

Blending time.

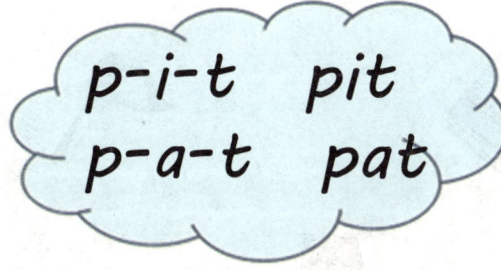

A. Let's learn.

N n
nose

n, n, N.
n, n, nose.

B. Let's trace, write and say.

N n

C. Listen and circle the words with the sound /n/.

1.  2.  3.

4.  5.

D. Let's chant and do.

I have a nose. *n-n-n*.

Look at my nose. *n-n-n*.

Touch my nose. *n-n-n*.

Hold my nose, achoo!

Action: Please point at your nose, and say *n, n, n*.

Revision 1

A. Match and write.

T   p

S   i

N   s

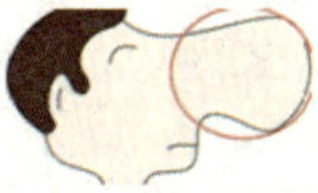

A   t

I   n

P   a

B. Let's blend.

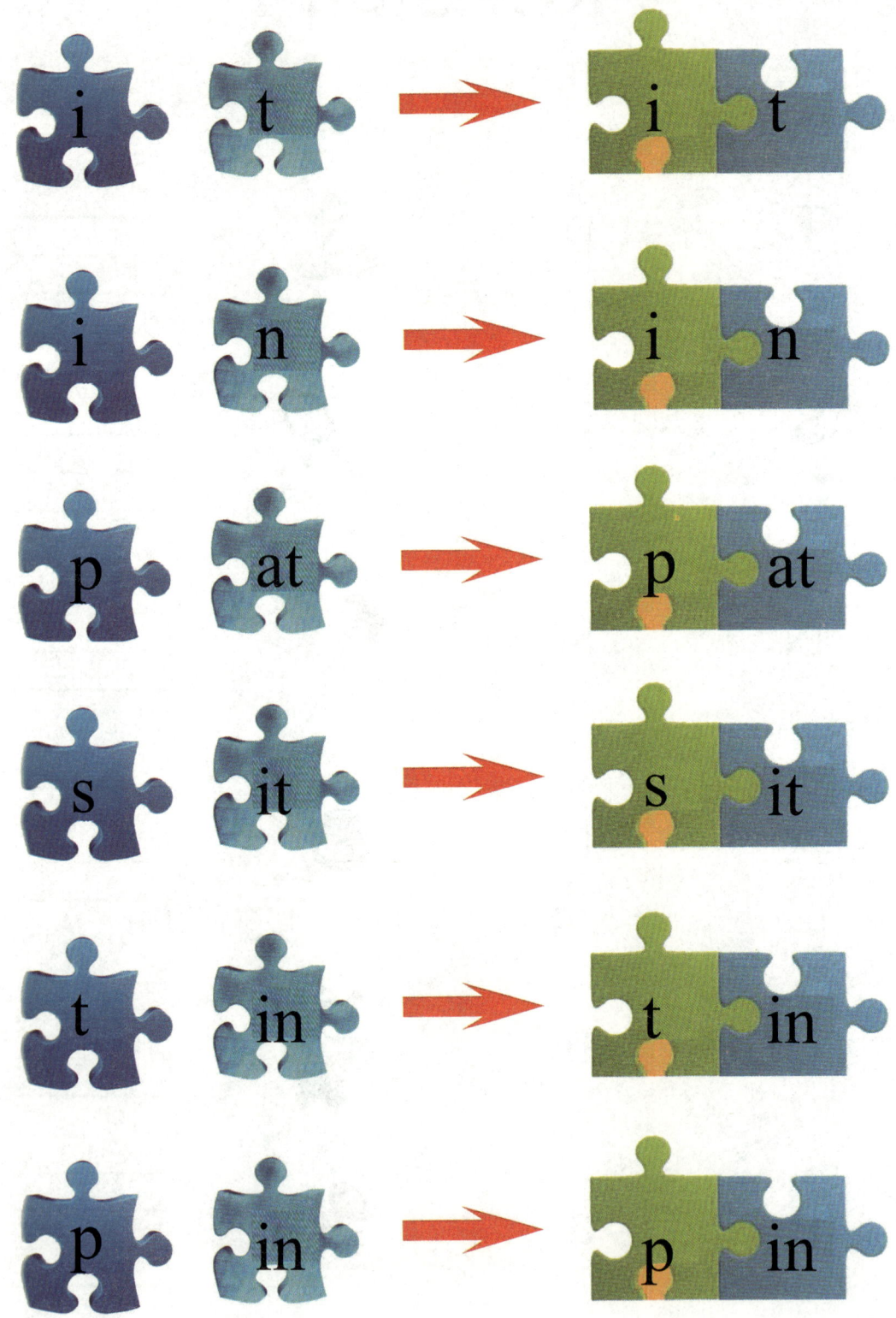

C. Let's read.

An ant.
An apple.
An ant sat on an apple.

A snake.
The sun.
A snake is in the sun.

Try to write:

        a   an

Try to talk:

A _____.
The _____.
A _____ is in the _____.

D. Let's play.

Unit 2 C K E H R M D

Blending time.

n-i-p   nip
t-i-n   tin

p-a-n   pan
n-a-p   nap

A. Let's learn.

Cc/Kk

kite

Cat

c, c, C. c, c, cat.
k, k, K. k, k, kite.

B. Let's trace, write and say.

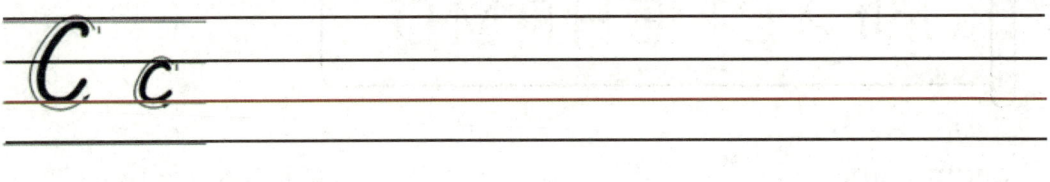

C. Listen and circle the words with the sound /k/.

1.    2.    3.

4.    5.

D. Let's chant and do.

Knock, knock, knock. k-k-k.
Knock, knock, knock. k-k-k.
Who is coming?
A cat is coming.
Knock, knock, knock. k-k-k.

Action: Pretend to be a cat, and knock at the door with your knuckles, saying k, k, k.

Unit 2 C K E H R M D

Blending time.

k-i-n kin
c-a-t cat

c-a-n can
k-i-p kip

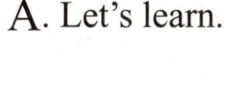

A. Let's learn.

E e
egg

e, e, E.
e, e, egg.

B. Let's trace, write and say.

C. Listen and circle the words with the sound /e/.

1.   2.   3.

4.   5.

D. Let's chant and do.

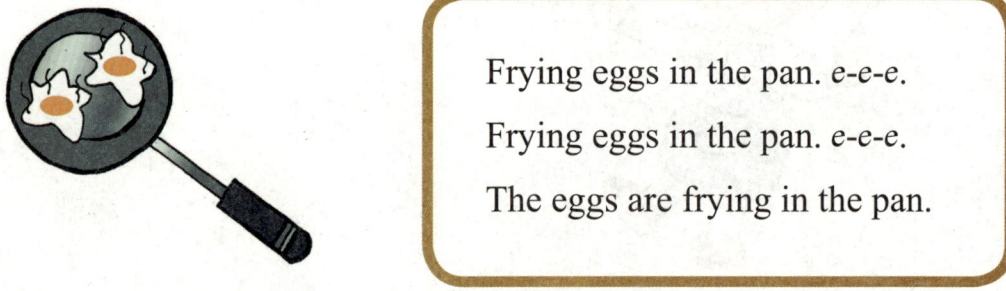

Frying eggs in the pan. *e-e-e*.
Frying eggs in the pan. *e-e-e*.
The eggs are frying in the pan.

Action: Please use your hands to break the egg shell, saying *e, e, e*.

Unit 2 C K E H R M D

Blending time.

n-e-t   net
s-e-t   set

p-e-t   pet
k-i-t   kit

A. Let's learn.

H h
hen

h, h, H.
h, h, hen.

B. Let's trace, write and say.

Hh

C. Write H h, then listen and match.

1. 　　2.

3. 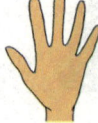　　4.

D. Let's chant and do.

Shake hands up. *h-h-h*.
Shake hands down. *h-h-h*.
Shake shake hands, turn around.
h-h-h.

Action: Shake your body up and down, then put your hands on your hips, panting as if you are out of breath, and say *h, h, h*.

Unit 2 C K E H R M D

Blending time.

h-i-p hip
h-e-n hen

s-i-p sip
c-a-t cat

A. Let's learn.

R r

rabbit

r, r, R.
r, r, rabbit.

B. Let's trace, write and say.

Rr

C. Look and write the missing letters.

1.  ed

2. red mouse at

3. rabbit abbit

4. girl running un

D. Let's chant and do.

Angry, angry.
The dog is angry. *r-r-r.*
Why is he so angry?
Because he is so hungry. *r-r-r.*

Action: Pretend to be an angry dog, shake your head from side to side, saying *r, r, r.*

Unit 2 C K E H R M D

Blending time.

A. Let's learn.

M m

mum

m, m, M.
m, m, Mum.

B. Let's trace, write and say.

C. Which one begins with the sound /m/ ? Listen and circle.

1.

2.

3.

D. Let's chant and do.

Mum makes a meal.
The meal tastes good! *m-m-m*.
The meal is great! *m-m-m*.
Yummy!

Action: Rub your tummy, as if you are full, and say *m, m, m*.

Unit 2 C K E H R M D

Blending time.

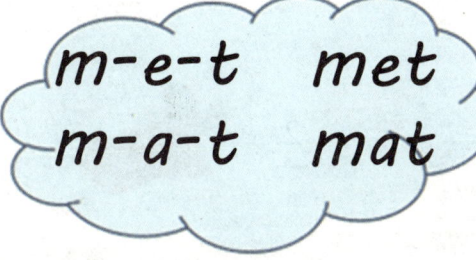

m-e-t   met
m-a-t   mat

r-a-t   rat
h-i-p   hip

A. Let's learn.

D d
dad

d, d, D.
d, d, dad.

B. Let's trace, write and say.

D d

C. Write D d, then listen and match.

1.

2.

3.

4.

D. Let's chant and do.

d-d-d, drum, *d-d-d*, drum.

Beat the drum, *d-d-d*.

Beat the drum, *d-d-d*.

Action: Pretend to be a drummer, beat your hands up and down, as if you are playing a drum, and say *d, d, d*.

Revision 2

A. Match and write.

H	e	(egg)	____
K	c	(dog)	____
D	r	(hen)	____
C	k	(mango)	____
M	h	(cat)	____
E	d	(rabbit)	____
R	m	(kite)	____

B. Let's blend.

C. Let's read.

An egg.
A pan.
An egg is in a pan.

A hen.
A den.
A hen is in a den.

Try to write:

                    is   in

Try to talk:

A _____.
A _____.
A _____.

D. Let's play.

Unit 3 G O U L F B

Blending time.

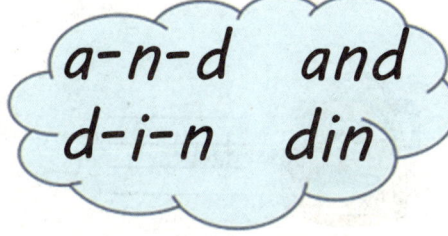

a-n-d and
d-i-n din

r-e-d red
d-a-t dat

A. Let's learn.

G g

gift

g, g, G.
g, g, gift.

B. Let's trace, write and say.

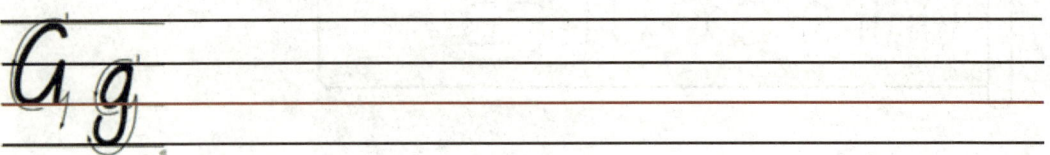

C. Listen and write the missing letters.

1. ift
2. ba
3. as
4. ood

D. Let's listen and do.

Get up, get up,
Time to get up.
Come on, let's go,
Let's go to play!
g-g-g, go! go! go!

Action: Pretend to walk on the sidewalk happily and say *g,g, g*.

Unit 3 G O U L F B

Blending time.

g-e-t get
g-a-s gas

d-i-g dig
r-a-g rag

A. Let's learn.

O o

orange

o, o, O.
o, o, orange.

B. Let's trace, write and say.

C. Write O o, then listen and match.

D. Let's listen and do.

Look at the dog.

It is hot.

o-o-o dog. *o-o-o* hot.

The dog is hot, very very hot.

Action: Pretend to be a puppy, stick out the tongue and say *o, o, o*.

Unit 3 G O U L F B

Blending time.

A. Let's learn.

U u
umbrella

u, u, U.
u, u, umbrella.

B. Let's trace, write and say.

C. Listen, match and write U u.

1.  2.  3.  4.

D. Let's listen and do.

Jump, jump, jump, *u-u-u*.

Up, up, up, *u-u-u*.

Jump up high.

Let me fly.

Action: Jump up high, stretch your arms and say *u, u, u*.

Unit 3 G O U L F B

Blending time.

m-u-g mug
r-u-n run

m-u-m mum
c-u-p cup

A. Let's learn.

L l

lollipop

l, l, L.
l, l, lollipop.

B. Let's trace, write and say.

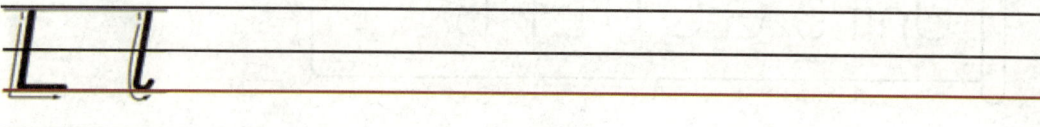

C. Write L l, then listen and match.

1.

2.    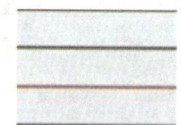   4.

3.

D. Let's listen and do.

I have a lollipop. *l-l-l*.

Look at my lollipop. *l-l-l*.

Lick my lollipop. *l-l-l*.

I love my lollipop. *l-l-l*.

Action: Hold out the thumb, pretend to lick the lollipop, and say *l, l, l*.

Unit 3 G O U L F B

Blending time.

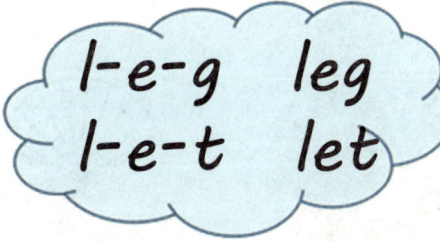

A. Let's learn.

F f

fish

f, f, F.
f, f, fish.

B. Let's trace, write and say.

C. Which ones begin with the sound /f/ ? Listen and colour.

1.  2.  3.

4.  5.  6.

D. Let's listen and do.

I went to the beach
with my floating fish.
It got a hole,
the air came out.
f-f-f.

Action: Let your hands come together gently. As if an inflatable fish is deflating, and say f, f, f.

Unit 3 G O U L F B

Blending time.

f-a-t   fat
f-u-n   fun

h-a-d   had
k-e-p   kep

A. Let's learn.

B b
ball

b, b, B.
b, b, ball.

B. Let's trace, write and say.

B b

C. Listen and write the missing letters.

1.  ed

2.  at

3. 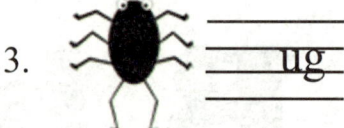 ug

4.  us

D. Let's listen and do.

Ball, ball, football.
Ball, ball, basketball.
b-b-b, ball, ball, ball.
Let's play with the ball.

Action: Pretend to bounce a ball, and say *b*, *b*, *b*.

Revision 3

A. Let's match.

B. Let's blend.

C. Let's read.

I see a man,
I see a bus.
I see a man in a bus.

I see an umbrella.
I see a desk.
I see an umbrella on a desk.

Try to write:

    I   see   on

Try to talk:

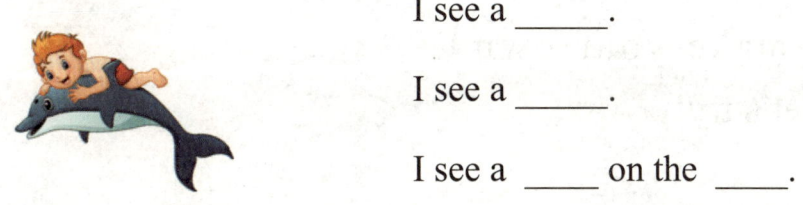

I see a _____.

I see a _____.

I see a ____ on the ____.

D. Let's play.

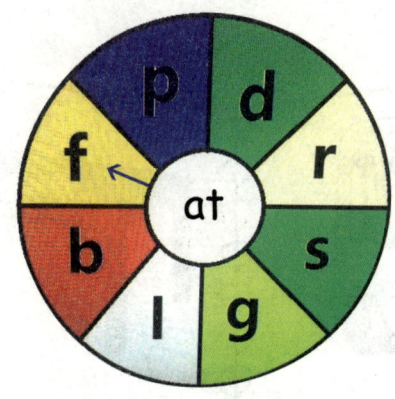

Look! Here's a spinner. Let's spin it and blend!

Can you make your own spinner? Let's try!

Unit 4 J Z W V Y X Q

Blending time.

b-a-g   bag
b-u-s   bus

f-a-t   fat
f-i-n   fin

A. Let's learn.

J j

jelly

j, j, J.
j, j, jelly.

B. Let's trace, write and say.

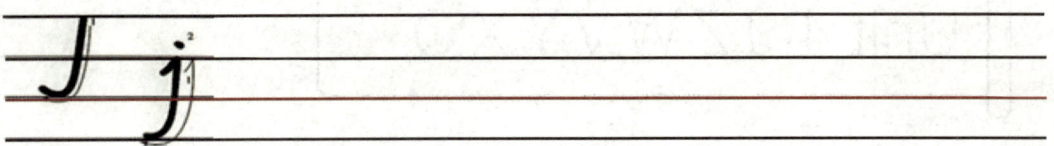

C. Listen and write J j.

1.   2.   3.

D. Let's listen and do.

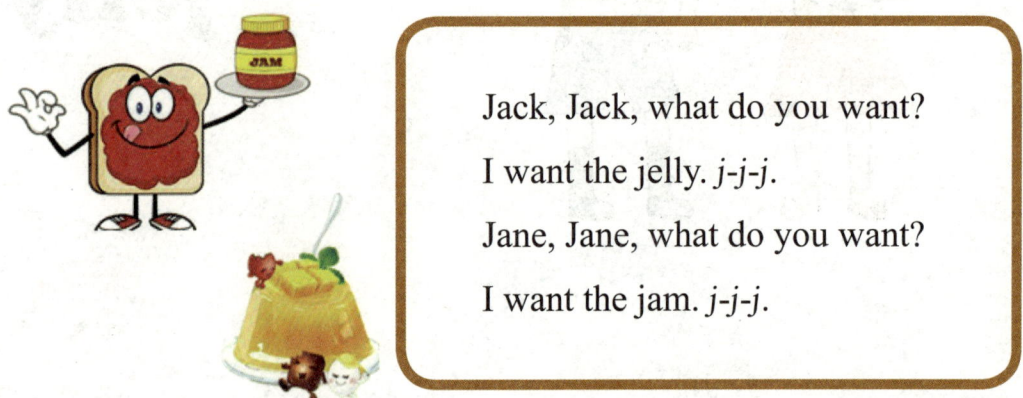

Jack, Jack, what do you want?

I want the jelly. *j-j-j*.

Jane, Jane, what do you want?

I want the jam. *j-j-j*.

Action: Smack lips, as if you want to eat jelly and jam, and say *j, j, j*.

Unit 4 J Z W V Y X Q

Blending time.

J-a-ck Jack
j-a-b jab

j-u-m-p jump
j-a-m jam

A. Let's learn.

Z z

zoo

z, z, Z.
z, z, zoo.

B. Let's trace, write and say.

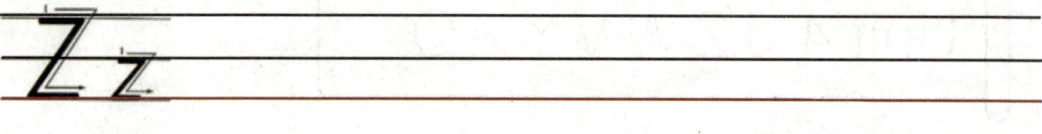

C. Write Z z, then listen and match.

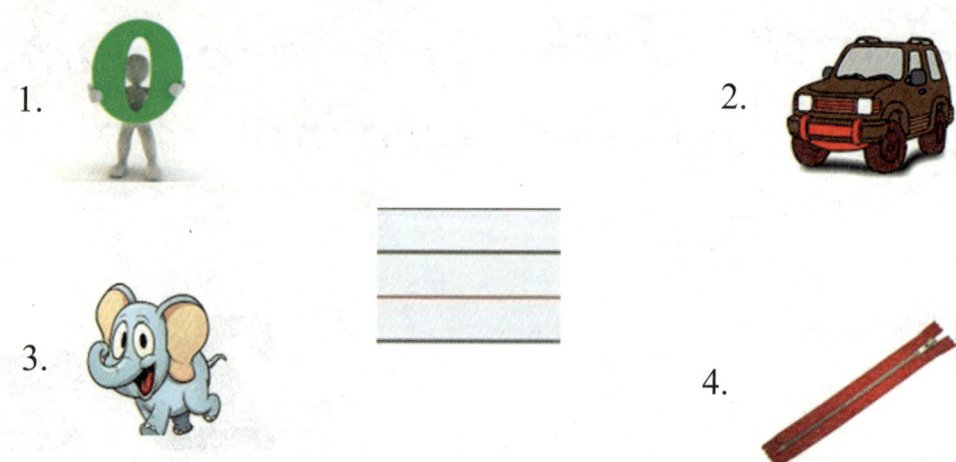

D. Let's listen and do.

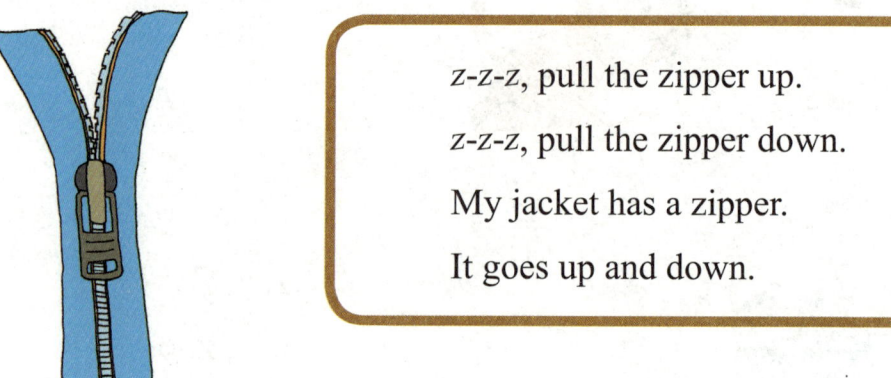

z-z-z, pull the zipper up.

z-z-z, pull the zipper down.

My jacket has a zipper.

It goes up and down.

Action: Pretend you have a zipper, and pull the zipper up and down, and say z, z, z.

Unit 4 J Z W V Y X Q

Blending time.

A. Let's learn.

Ww
window

w, w, W.
w, w, window.

B. Let's trace, write and say.

C. Let's listen and circle the words with the sound /w/.

1.    2.    3.

4.    5.

D. Let's listen and do.

Wind, wind, wind,
The wind is blowing.
w-w-w, w-w-w.
Winter is coming.

Action: Blow with your mouth, as if the wind is blowing, and say w, w, w.

Unit 4 J Z W V Y X Q

Blending time.

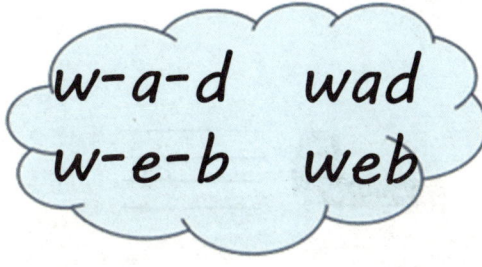

A. Let's learn.

V v
van

v, v, V.
v, v, van.

B. Let's trace, write and say.

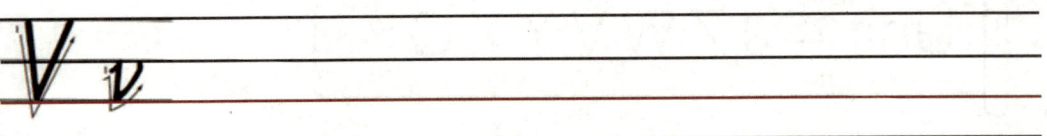

C. Read the words, then write the missing letters.

___est   ___an

___et   ___as

D. Let's listen and do.

v-v-v, drive my van.

v-v-v, drive my van.

A fast van.

I'm a mail man.

Action: Pretend to be driving a van fast, saying v, v, v.

Unit 4 J Z W V Y X Q

Blending time.

v-e-t   vet
w-i-g   wig

z-i-p   zip
j-e-t   jet

A. Let's learn.

Y y

yogurt

y, y, Y.
y, y, yogurt.

B. Let's trace, write and say.

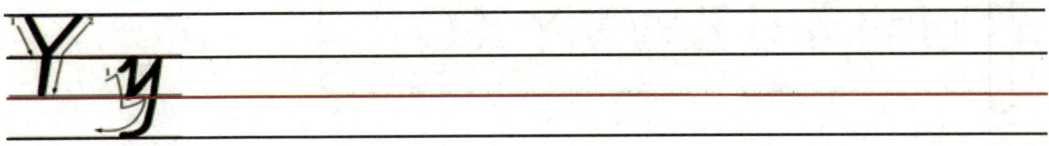

C. Write Y y, then listen and match.

D. Let's listen and do.

y-y-y, yummy, yummy, yummy.

The yogurt is yummy.

y-y-y, yucky, yucky, yucky.

The bug is yucky.

Action: Pretend to eat delicious yogurt and say y, y, y with a smile face, and eat disgusting bug and say y, y, y with a sad face.

Unit 4 JZWVYXQ

Blending time.

A. Let's learn.

X x
X-ray

x, x, X.
x, x, X-ray.

B. Let's trace, write and say.

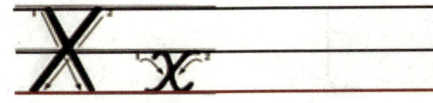

C. Listen and write X x.

1.    2.    3.    4.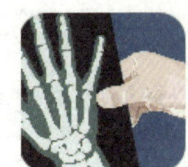

D. Let's listen and do.

x-x-x, box.
x-x-x, fox.
Where is the fox?
It's in the box.

Action: Pretend to be a fox climbing a box with the sound *x, x, x*.

Unit 4 J Z W V Y X Q

Blending time.

s-i-x six
f-o-x fox

y-e-n yen
w-e-t wet

A. Let's learn.

Q q
queen

qu qu, Q.
qu, qu, queen.

B. Let's trace, write and say.

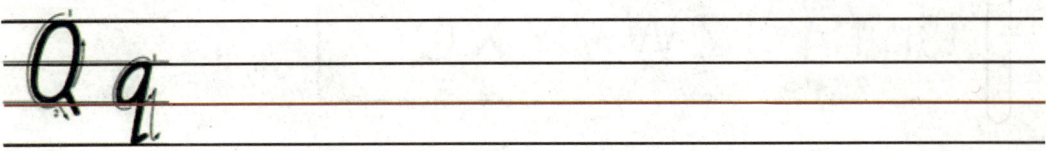

C. Listen and circle the words with the sound /kw/, then write Q q.

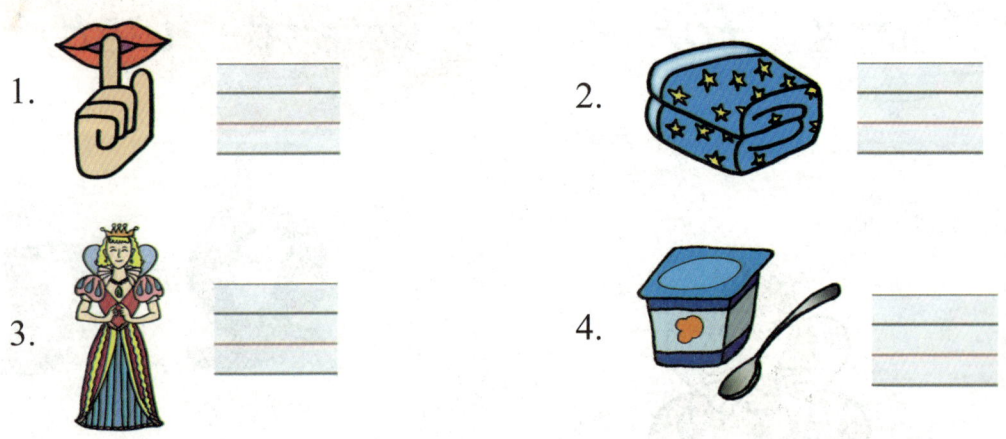

1.   2.

3.   4.

D. Let's listen and do.

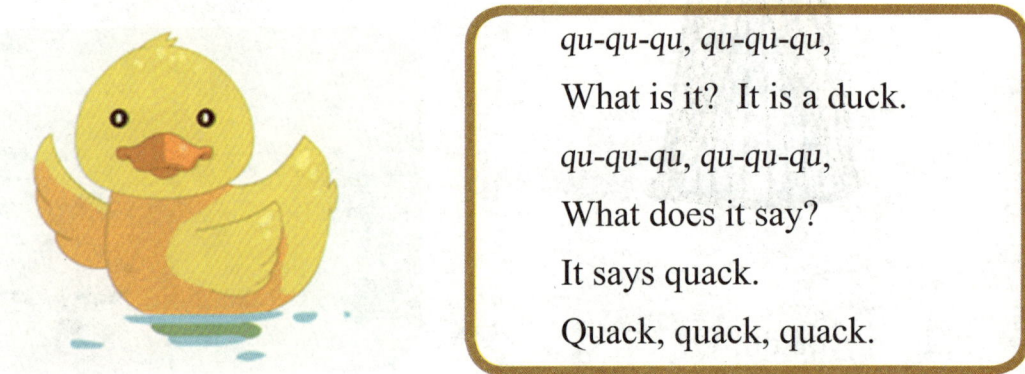

qu-qu-qu, qu-qu-qu,
What is it? It is a duck.
qu-qu-qu, qu-qu-qu,
What does it say?
It says quack.
Quack, quack, quack.

Action: Pretend to be a duck and say *qu, qu, qu*.

Revision 4

A. Let's match.

B. Let's blend.

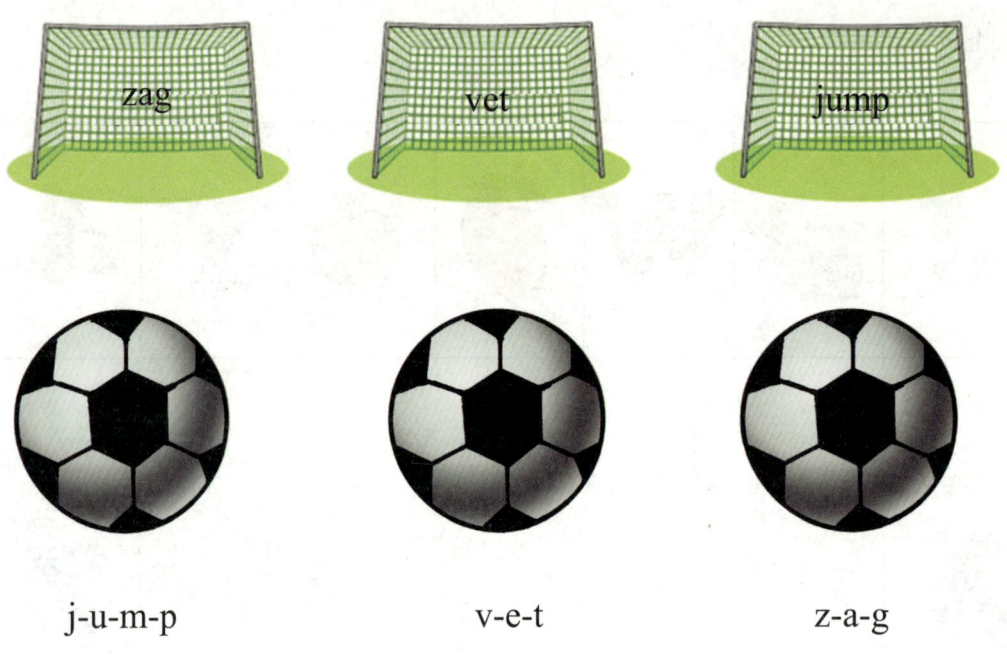

j-u-m-p   v-e-t   z-a-g

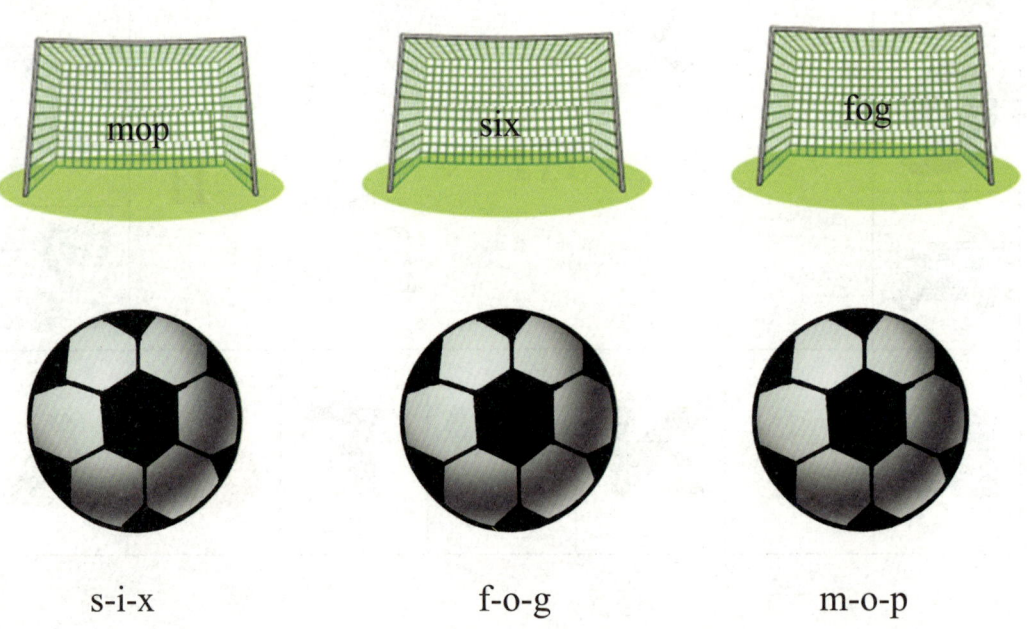

s-i-x   f-o-g   m-o-p

C. Let's read.

I like the milk.
I like the jug.
I like the milk in the jug.

I like the dog.
I like the mud.
I like dog in the mud.

Try to write:

                like   the

Try to talk:

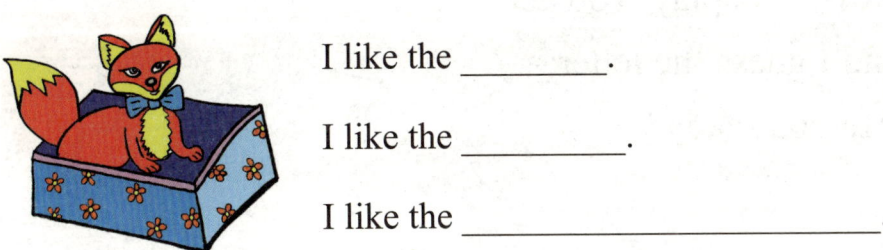

I like the _____.

I like the _____.

I like the _____.

D. Let's play.

Finger Letters

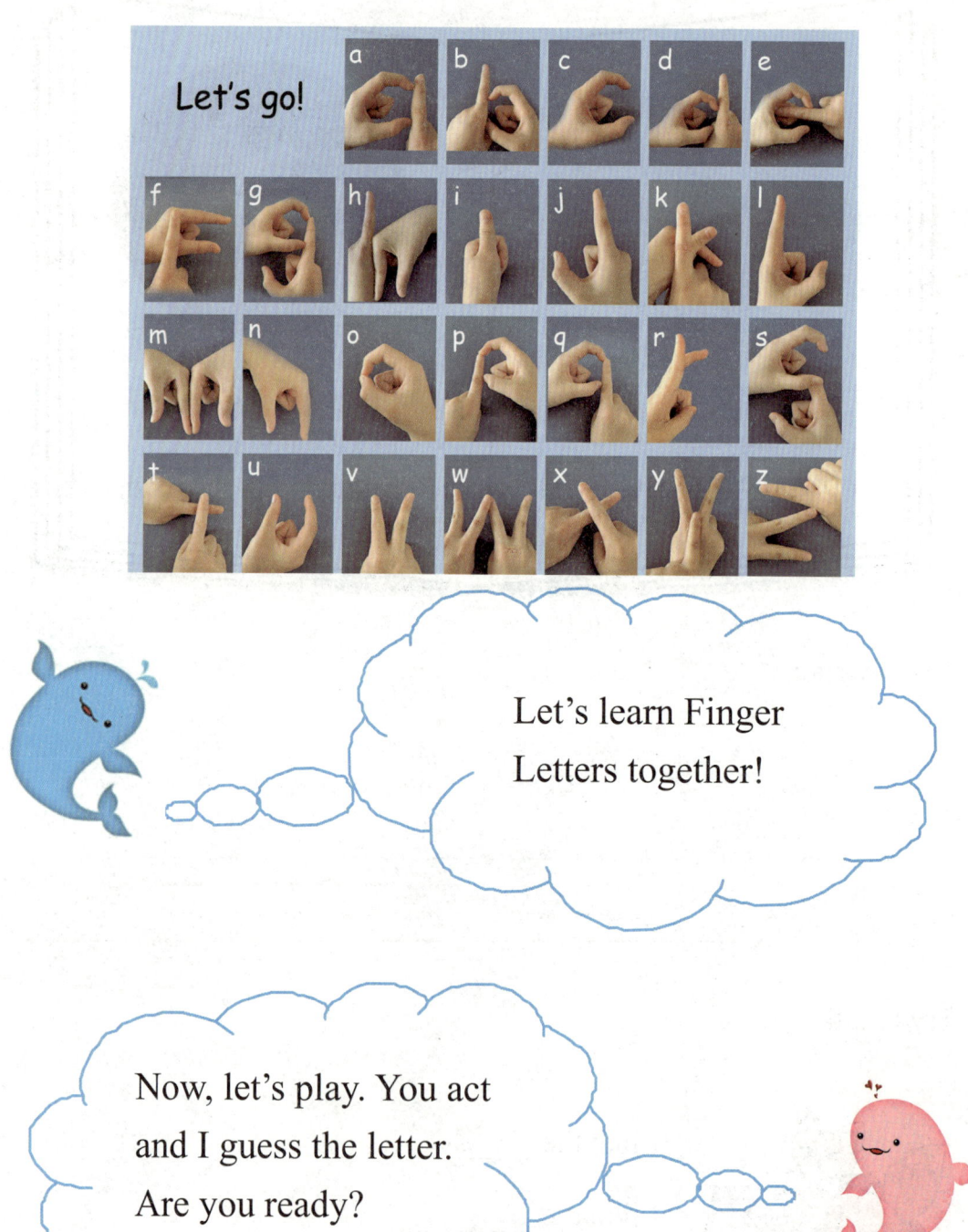

Let's learn Finger Letters together!

Now, let's play. You act and I guess the letter. Are you ready?

Read for Fun

Let's Be Friends!

Hello, I am Blue.
I am six.
I live in China.

Hi, my name is Pink.
I am five.
I live in the Yangtze River.

We like to play in the river.
We like to smile.
Let's be friends!